AFRICA

BY MARY LINDEEN

Africa is the second-largest **continent** in the world. The Atlantic Ocean is west of Africa. The Indian Ocean is east of Africa. Europe is north of Africa.

Africa is one of seven continents on Earth.

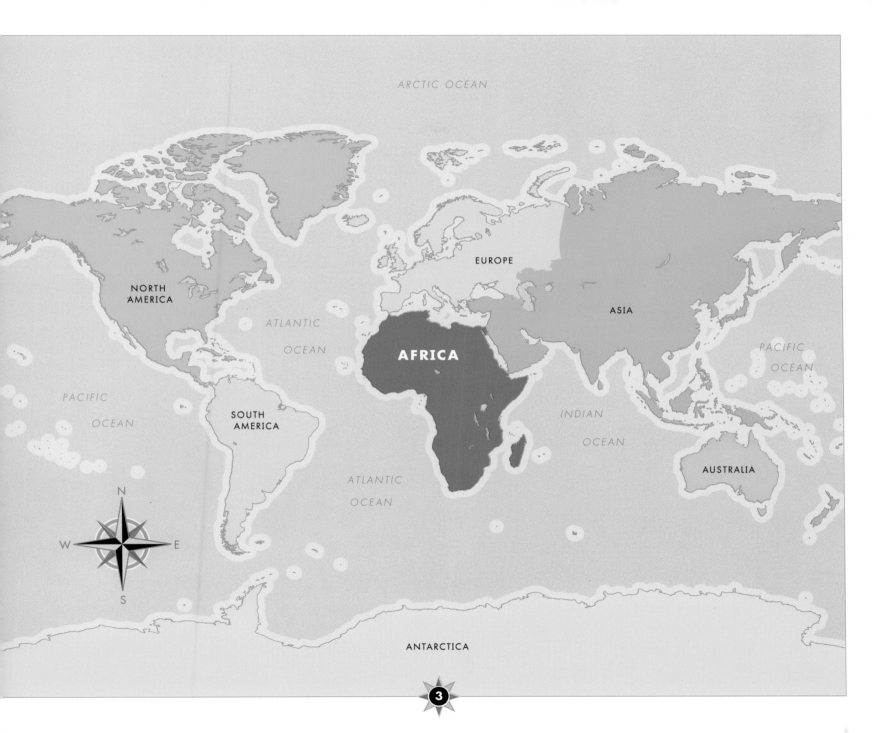

ARCTIC OCEAN

EUROPE

NORTH
AMERICA

ATLANTIC

OCEAN

AFRICA

ASIA

PACIFIC

OCEAN

PACIFIC

OCEAN

SOUTH
AMERICA

INDIAN

OCEAN

ATLANTIC

OCEAN

AUSTRALIA

N

W   E

S

ANTARCTICA

Most of the land in Africa is hot and flat. Some of the land is desert. The largest desert in the world is in Africa. It is called the Sahara.

 The Sahara is about the same size as the United States.

Some of the land in Africa is **rain forest**. Many rare animals live in the rain forest.

African grey parrots are rare. They live in some of Africa's rain forests.

Some of Africa's land is open and grassy. This is called the **savanna**. Many animals live on the savanna.

☞ Zebras and elephants live on the African savanna.

There are many **countries** in Africa. There are all kinds of people. Some people wear colorful clothes and jewelry.

Members of the Masai (mah-SY) tribe are known for their colorful clothing.

Many people in Africa are farmers.

They grow coffee, cocoa, fruits, and

other crops.

 These farmers in Rwanda are growing corn.

Some people in Africa live in the desert.

Some of their homes are made of mud

and straw.

Mud huts are common in some areas of Africa. These huts are in Namibia.

Some people live in big cities by rivers, lakes, and the ocean. The largest city in Africa is Cairo (KY-roh), Egypt.

 Cairo is home to more than nine million people.

A lot of people live along the Nile River.

It is the longest river in the world.

Some people fish on the Nile River.

There are many beautiful places to see in Africa. What would you plan to see there?

 Victoria Falls is in Africa. It is one of the largest waterfalls in the world.

GLOSSARY

continent (KON-tuh-nent): A continent is one of seven large land areas on Earth. Africa is a continent.

countries (KUN-trees): Countries are areas of land with their own governments. Egypt is one of many countries in Africa.

rain forest (RAYN FOR-ist): A rain forest is a hot forest where a lot of rain falls. Millions of kinds of animals and insects live in the rain forest.

savanna (suh-VAN-uh): A savanna is a flat, grassy plain with few trees found in warm areas. Giraffes and zebras live on the African savanna.

TO FIND OUT MORE

Books

Gagne, Tammy. *The Nile River*. Hockessin, DE: Mitchell Lane Publishers, 2013.

Hirsch, Rebecca. *Africa*. New York, NY: Scholastic, 2013.

Orr, Tamra B. *The Animals of Africa*.
Kennett Square, PA: Purple Toad Publishing, 2017.

Web Sites

Visit our Web site for links about Africa:

childsworld.com/links

Note to Parents, Teachers, and Librarians: We routinely verify our Web links to make sure
they are safe and active sites. So encourage your readers to check them out!

INDEX

The Child's World®
childsworld.com

Published by The Child's World®
1980 Lookout Drive • Mankato, MN 56003-1705
800-599-READ • www.childsworld.com

Credits: Andrzej Kubik/Shutterstock.com: 8; astudio/
Shutterstock.com: 4; Elina Litovkina/cover, 1; jaja/Shutterstock.
com: 19; Matt Elliott/Shutterstock: 20; meunierd/Shutterstock.
com: 11, 15; Nichcha1911/Shutterstock.com: 7; Orhan Cam/
Shutterstock.com: 16; wlablack/Shutterstock.com: 12

ISBN HARDCOVER: 9781503824935
ISBN PAPERBACK: 9781622434145
LCCN: 2017960455

Printed in the United States of America • PA02372

ABOUT THE AUTHOR

Mary Lindeen is an elementary school teacher who turned her love
of children and books into a career in publishing. She has written and
edited many library books and literacy programs. She also enjoys
traveling with her son, Benjamin, whenever and wherever she can.

On the cover: The African savanna has warm weather all year round.